From Dirt to Pearl

A Woman's Traumatic Story of Neglect,
Abuse, Betrayal, Murder, and Survival.
How God has Transformed my Life.

Monica Lasha Lane

ISBN 978-1-0980-6180-7 (paperback)
ISBN 978-1-0980-6181-4 (digital)

Christian Faith Publishing, Inc.
832 Park Avenue
Meadville, PA 16335
www.christianfaithpublishing.com

Printed in the United States of America

The country music song that says, "What doesn't kill you makes you stronger" is very appropriate for my life. As I look back on my life, it is not always with fond memories, but I can see my heavenly Father watching over me every step of the way. Not many people can recall being watched over by angels while being shot at by automatic weapons, but that story is for a later time.

My earliest memory at age three is the feeling of fear as I was left at the home of my oldest brother's grandmother. My mother, Eddie Mae, had issues, which made it difficult for her to raise her children. Contrary to some beliefs, public assistance doesn't pay for many things such as clothing and utilities. There are other reasons, one of which is just pure selfishness. It is easy to conceive a child but very difficult to raise them, especially when you don't have a support system, namely a husband, to help you with the day-to-day responsibilities.

My memories of those first years are scattered, but I do remember my mother telling me that I was going to live with my father's family in Marion, Alabama. I had an older sister, Della, who was already being raised by our grandmother. Praise God for that time because for the first time, I felt loved and cherished by my grandmother Sarah King and my Aunts Shirley, Annie, Daisy and Betty. They even helped raise my dad's first wife Sander's children who were my stepsisters. My cousin, Katrian, stayed every summer with us, and we are still great friends today.

My grandmother would press and curl my hair and dress me like a princess every day. She wouldn't even let me go outside alone to use the outhouse. I had my own chamber pot to use to which she added Pine Sol or bleach to kill the germs. We were poor, but we were rich in God's love.

The King family knew God and served him daily. My grandmother knew how to pray, and she did it with fervor. I remember her telling me that God will never leave you and will protect you, no matter what happens. Her words have stayed with me my whole life.

Now you may be wondering about my father, Judge King. I was born in 1972, which was a difficult time for racial relations in the South. Marion, Alabama, was certainly no exception. Judge King was active in the Civil Rights movement with the late Dr. Martin Luther King Jr. from 1955 until he was assassinated in 1968. Dad was involved in the Bloody Sunday that happened in Selma in March 7, 1965. He has never talked about this time, and I didn't know about it until I was grown. He has always been a part of my life, and I cherish him and his love. African American men don't always admit that they have fathered children. My dad is an exception.

During this time, I loved going to school and church. Family and friends served God and each other. I couldn't wait to absorb what the world had to offer. I was loved and protected. What more could a child want?

2

My blessed childhood changed when I was around nine years old. My mother came to get me and took me home with her. This is when the dark chapter of my life began. We lived on Patton Avenue which is just off Martin Luther King Avenue (formerly Davis Avenue) in Mobile, Alabama. I have many stressful memories of this time. My hair would be so ugly because no one would take the time to comb it. My brother, Carlos, and I would miss the school bus often because we didn't want anyone to see us.

I remember this man that was going with my mom, saying, "You better not let them boys be playing with you." Until this time, I had been raised in a Christian household. I trusted people and had no idea what went on with adults. When grown-ups started talking, children went to another room or outside, playing. I trusted people, but that was soon to change.

One day, the man told me to go into the room, and he would be in there to check me and make sure that no one was messing with me. I remember saying, "No, my mom is not here, and I will let her talk to me about this."

He began to say, "You can talk to me about this. I talked to your mom about it already."

At this point, I didn't know what to believe. I didn't really know him or my mother. I saw that I didn't have a choice in the matter.

He said he had to check me to see if boys had been messing with me. Then he took Vaseline and put it on my private parts and raped me. When he finished raping me, he cleaned the blood off of me and told me to take a bath before my mother got home. At the time, I had no idea that I had been raped. He led me to believe that what he did was normal.

Another day, my mother left me and my brother, Carlos, with him. He told Carlos to go outside because he needed me to do something inside. I asked my little brother not to leave, but the man insisted that he go outside. Carlos had no idea of what was going on either.

After this, I told my mother that the man was doing bad things to me. The only thing she would say was, "Stop telling lies. You just want to be grown or go back with your dad. You are not going back with those people."

Shortly after this time, my dad came to Mobile to see me. My mother had warned me to not tell my dad about the abuse because if I did, I would get a butt-whipping and never see my dad again. When my dad would start to leave, I would run behind the car, begging for him to not leave me with these people. He would say, "This is your family too. You have to stay here."

The verbal and sexual abuse continued. My brother asked me once why I was so angry all the time, and I would say nothing. One night, my mother left to go to work at a nightclub and left us with the man. He told me to go into the bathroom because he needed to check me out, and my mother came back because she forgot something. He told her that I had done something and that he was going to whip me, and that is why I was in the bathroom. She never once asked what I did. She just believed him. My little brother was on the other side of the house and never knew anything was happening.

I found comfort in being able to visit in other people's homes in the neighborhood. I have forgotten a lot of the names, but I remember Mrs. Fay fondly. She had a son named Rock, but she took up a lot of time with me also. She would sit me down and teach me to say my ABCs and read. She would tell me, "You are a pretty girl and you need to learn to read because that will take you a long way in life." I thank God for Mrs. Fay.

One day, I hit myself in the eye with a stick in front of Mrs. Fay's house, and my eye was bleeding. She wanted to take me to the doctor, but I cried and begged not to go. I thought that if I went to the doctor that they could tell what the man was doing to me, and then he would really hurt me. I feel that she sensed what was happening because she would ask me frequently how I was doing and if things were okay at home. I never told her the truth, but I think she suspected that I was being abused.

About the time that I turned ten, my grandmother Irma, who was raising my sister, Della, found out that I was being abused. It was then that I learned that the reason Della was not staying with us was because she had been abused also. The marks of that abuse on beautiful Della influenced the rest of her short life.

Many arguments between my mother and grandmother marked the next few months. My mother could no longer deny my being abused, so she decided that we needed to move. She continued to verbally abuse me, saying that I was trying to be grown, and that is why her boyfriend raped me. She never listened, so I didn't respond.

We moved to a place in Mobile, Alabama, called Trinity Gardens. Tragedy hit soon after. Carlos and I were playing with fire, and we burned the house down. She beat us terribly for that. I don't think that my mother ever realized that you are supposed to watch children with a loving eye.

After that, we moved around the corner, and things got much better for a short while. It was just the three of us. We were able to go out and play with the neighborhood children.

Then she started to leave us with a lady down the street who had a son who also molested me. By this time, I believed that no one would believe me. I was told all the time to stop lying when I was telling the truth. I was starting to mature physically, but emotionally, I was a wreck. I would cry every night until I fell asleep.

We moved again to another street in Trinity Gardens, and that is when things started to get really crazy again. By then, I knew that my mother only cared for herself. An old boyfriend from the past moved in, and he was a child molester also. He would touch me inappropriately and tell me how fine I was. No matter what I told my mother, she would say that I was lying. I always felt like I didn't have a childhood, that I was pushed into adulthood at a very early age.

Christmas was not a happy memory for us. Mother never gave us anything. When friends would give us presents, she would hide them. One day, her friend found the gifts and gave them to us. At least someone wanted us to be happy.

3

In 1986, I met my oldest brother on the school bus. I had no idea that he existed. We had the same mother. Thank God we didn't date. He asked me where I was from, and I told him Trinity Gardens, and he said that he had family there. I asked him who, and he said, "I have a brother named Carlos and a sister named Della Mechelle and another named Monica. My name is Edley, and my mother's name is Eddie Mae Lane."

It was like something out of a movie. We got off the bus at his grandmother's house, and he showed me all kinds of pictures of us when we were little. In looking back, I wonder what would have happened if someone had just reported all this craziness to the welfare system. But my mother was an expert liar. She would probably have lied her way out of this like she had always done before. All I and my brothers and sisters needed was anyone who would care enough to break this chain of sin, neglect, and abuse.

God was always there, just waiting on someone to pick up an ax and break the chain with his help. I needed someone to love me, so I started seeking love in all the wrong places instead of turning to God. Thank God he is with me now.

After that good news, at the age of fifteen, I had a baby girl—my own live baby doll. My mother was mad, but I was happy because

I finally had someone to love me. It was a difficult pregnancy and delivery, and I had to have a C-section.

What an environment for a young child. No wonder she had so many emotional problems later on. I loved that child with my whole heart and still do. But looking back, I realized that I was still a child myself and seriously needed help. I didn't get that help and continued to live as if there was no tomorrow.

Mother continued to verbally abuse both Carlos and myself. She would steal things and blame me or Carlos. I fought back by stealing her car and taking it for joyrides. I just wanted to go live with my dad or grandmother. She would beat me and tell me that I wasn't going anywhere.

When I was sixteen, I was sitting and talking with a guy named Anthony. My mother came up and told me that she had better not see me talking to him again. When I got back to my house, she put a gun to my head and told me that she would kill me. That was when I decided I had to move out of her house.

I ran away from home and didn't look back. I had to leave my daughter with her at first, but after a short while, my friend, Anthony, and I saw her in the backyard, and we took her with us.

My dear friend, Anthony, had his own share of tragedies. Because of his problems, he understood what I had been through. We were still so young, and he fell in love with a young lady. After a tumultuous relationship, he shot his child's mother and her boyfriend and then shot himself. He was such a strong person, but after a very difficult childhood, he couldn't take anymore grief. Perhaps if he had a relationship with God at an early age as I did, he and his family would still be alive.

At this point, I had no one and no place to go, so I moved in with this guy named Al. He was very controlling and didn't want anyone around me. I finally got away from him with God's help, but my child and I had to live in my car for a while. It was like two kids with no place to go. We would be there at night and play in the park all day. About a year later, I found out that Al had been shot and killed in Prichard. Tragedy seemed to follow me everywhere.

I finally broke down and asked my mother to keep my child so that I could go to school. I thought that she was a changed person when she asked to keep her on the weekend. Because I didn't come and get her when I said that I would, she put my baby on the front porch and left her there. I found her after I got in from school on Monday. It was cold, and I was so mad. At this time, I was still seeking my own way instead of relying on God, and life was out of control. I tried taking her to school with me but, of course, that didn't work. Where were the school counselors? How many young girls today could benefit from a helping hand and stop the cycle of poverty and abuse?

It was another guy name Mike, but he moved out of town with his father. So I contacted Eddie who I think is her father and asked him to help me with the baby. He would keep her during the day and bring her to school to see me at lunch. Nothing seemed to last for me, and his family moved out of town. There I was again, alone without anyone to depend upon.

My Aunt Shirley came to rescue me again and started to help take care of the baby. I went back to school, but I was so far behind that I dropped out and got a job. *Depression* is a mild word for what I was going through at that time. My aunt kept my oldest for several years.

In looking back, I see how easy it is to blame a teenage mother for her behavior. The questions that remain unanswered are, "What caused that behavior in the first place? And what can be done to stop this behavior?"

To make matters even worse, I found out that I was pregnant again. So at this time, I moved in with my dad and his girlfriend, but that didn't work out either. I started GED school and moved in with my cousin. That lasted a short while, and I started working on getting my own apartment. Because I was homeless and had two children, I was given priority, but I had to wait until I turned nineteen to qualify. I was so excited to have my own home until I found out where the apartment was located.

The apartment was in Happy Hills, which was the Josephine Allen Project. Happy Hills is a misnomer for the place because it was the most dangerous place to live in Mobile County. Violence was a daily occurrence in that project. Even the police don't want to go in there.

Then I started thanking God for the opportunity to have my own apartment. It was security that I had not known since I left my family in Marion, Alabama. Terry Figare and I moved in together and started having more babies. He was a good man and took good care of all of us. The problem was that I was using God as a sideline. If things were going bad, I sought him. Otherwise, if things were good, I was depending on myself. I see that behavior in myself and many people today.

Everything was fine until I decided that I wanted to go out and party. All hell broke loose, and our relationship started deteriorating. It wasn't long after that Terry started seeing someone else. We had these problems before and we would do things to spite each other. We were still children acting like children, but we had children. I found out when his aunt called me and said that he was seeing her friend. To this day, I don't know why she told me about the affair.

It was during this difficult time that my oldest daughter started displaying mental and emotional problems. She started telling lies about anything and everything. She said that she heard voices in her head that told her to do these things. She couldn't get along with anyone at school, and someone from the school would bring her home at 11:00 a.m. This behavior continued until high school. There wasn't a day that wasn't lived without drama. She told people that she was pregnant by my other children's father. After I had that proven as false, then she told my aunt that I wasn't taking care of her, anything to cause trouble so that she could be the center of attention.

I look back on this period in my life and wonder how I lived through it. One time, the oldest pushed baby doll, who was nine months old, down twelve stairs while she was in her walker. God intervened, and she came out the door in the walker. Spanking didn't seem to stop her from harming her siblings.

Another time, she cut Moo Moo's finger with a knife. Blood was everywhere. She also tried to kill Punkin by putting a plastic bag over his head while he was in the bathtub. I was beginning to notice that she never tried to hurt Nika, the middle child. She said repeatedly that she wanted to be the only child.

I was finally able to get help from the system. The social workers told me to get all the knives out of the house and provided counseling for everyone who needed it. I was a young mother, and this was a lot for me to handle. Many times, I wanted to kill myself and end it all. But God was always there to pick me back up. It takes all you can to live right, but it is so much easier if you trust God every step of the way. The flesh wants to do what is worldly. I had to work day and night to provide for my kids. I prayed constantly that God would lead me how to raise my kids. I had to watch other women with their children for guidance. It is bad when you don't know how to be a mother, but with God, all things are possible.

God has protected me so many times, most people can't believe the life I have had. When I was straying from God, I would go to clubs with different men. Numerous times, I had to hide behind a car to avoid getting hit from stray bullets.

My sister, Della, was having her own problems during this time. With a childhood similar to mine, it was no wonder that she turned to drugs. She had children that I had to take care of often because there was no one else to help her. She would get mad about all of her problems, and I would tell her to pray, and God would help her. Her reply was always, "I am not like you."

This discussion will always be remembered. She asked me to not get upset, but she had something to tell me. After I promised her that I wouldn't get upset, she told me that she was HIV positive. I had heard about this on TV but really didn't understand what was happening. As badly as I wanted to cry, I didn't, and I promised to protect her and her kids, which I did. She was a strong black woman and didn't even know it.

It took me years to understand why she said that she wasn't like me. I finally came to understand that she was saying, "I don't know how to let God take control. I am not as strong as you are."

I would tell her, "I am not as strong as you think I am. I give my problems to God."

Once again, I remember my grandmother King and the foundation that she gave me of trust in the Lord. Della missed that early knowledge of God and what he can do in our lives if we only have faith in him.

Terry and I had three children together. After we broke up, my friend, Maybelline, asked me if I would like to meet her friend, Carl. We dated for a while. I kept his children, and he cared for mine. We decided to move in together and get out of Happy Hills. My cousin was against this idea but didn't really tell me a reason. I should have listened. His former girlfriend was not ready to let him go.

We got a lease on a house with both our names. The former girlfriend started giving us a lot of problems. Apparently, she wanted Carl back and would go to any length to accomplish that. One day, she called me and described everything in our house from the color of the furniture to where the fish tank stood.

I wouldn't let Carl in that afternoon and confronted him through the front door. He denied having a relationship with her and said that my brother had brought her there. I might have believed him if I had any faith in people, especially men.

The devil had his way with me that day. I wouldn't let Carl in that day and told him to leave. He said, "I am not going to leave you or lose you."

I asked him to leave once again, and he said no and broke the window in the house to get in. I started running behind him with a two-by-four board and fell in a hole and crushed my ankle and broke it in three places. I stayed in the hospital for about two weeks. It was just God's protection that kept me from hitting Carl. I could still be in prison today for hurting him.

He came in several times in the hospital and asked me to come back to him, but I refused. He also wouldn't let anyone else take care of the children. His ex-girlfriend continued to mess with me. When I asked Carl to get her to leave me alone, he said, "She is not doing anything to you. You are tripping."

I said, "Okay, if you won't stop her, I will." I am not proud of the fact that I went to her work and asked her to come out, and she refused. She was driving the car that I had helped him get painted white and gold. I cut the tires and the top because I was tired of her picking on me and being betrayed by him.

He called my mother and told her that she would be putting flowers on my grave. I called him back and told him not to call her anymore. It was all his fault anyway. So I had to start all over.

I was homeless again. I started dating this guy and moved in with him and his mom. The problem was that I had more kids and no car, so it only lasted a week. I started "couch hopping," moving from place to place and hotel to hotel.

God led me to a small house in Trinity Gardens, and it was wonderful because it was just me and the kids. God has always led a way for us.

It was during this time that I met my friend, Bubba Nack. He was very protective of our family. In fact, one time, a guy we knew tried to harm my baby, and he intervened. I learned then that sometimes friends are more reliable than family. Months after that, he got shot five times, and his friend was killed. I stayed by his bedside and prayed that he would make it, and he did. Even when he told me to leave, I realized that he was just mad. I can't tell his testimony; he would have to do that. All I say is that God is good.

Bubba moved us in with him and his mom after he got out of the hospital, and we stayed there for about four months. After that, he and I went our separate ways.

Next, we moved to Orange Grove, which is another project in downtown Mobile. In fact, it is close to the Mobile River and was known for flooding, especially during hurricanes.

We experienced the flooding firsthand. One morning, we woke up, and the kids said, "Mama, the rain is in the house."

I was half asleep and soon, as I opened my eyes, I saw that water was everywhere. I called 911, and they said to keep the doors closed and get to a higher level. The kids were afraid, and so was I.

We were rescued once again by my friend and upstairs neighbor, Joan, when she and her kid's father took us upstairs with them. After that, we went to a shelter for people who had lost everything during that storm. I thank God for the people who were in place to help us.

6

It took some time, but they paid us well for us to move to a new place. After cleaning the apartment up good, we moved to Trinity Gardens again. This time, I had more children to look after. I rented a two-bedroom house. My cousin, Claudia, helped me with babysitting, and she was like my ride or die girl. One night, we went to the little club down the street, and that turned out to be a mistake. My old boyfriend, Carl, was there and got in a fight with the guy who I was seeing at the time. I called the police, and they picked up both of them. Carl asked me not to testify, but the police said that I had to. Carl got really mad again about the fact that I testified, so I was forced to move again. I went homeless, sleeping here and there again.

I went to my mom, and that, as usual, was a mistake. I found a place in Prichard called Snug Harbor. It was really cheap, like $99 to move in. It was there that I met Michael, also known as Pooh. After we had been seeing each other for about two months, someone told me that he was married. I had a hard time believing this, but I finally confronted him, and he admitted it. He said that they had a son together right out of high school and they had recently married. I told him to leave and make his marriage work.

One night, there was a knock at the door at about two in the morning. It was his friend, Pat, and she asked me if I had company, and I told her no. She asked if Smack (that was Pooh's nickname also) could come in and talk to me. So I talked to him, and he said that he loved me and wanted to be with me. I told him no because he married that woman for whatever reason, and I told him to live with her. He said that he had moved back in with his mom. I told him that I couldn't do that because it wasn't right. But after a time, we started seeing each other again. After about six months of him going back and forth between me and his mom, we moved in together in a place called Happy Hills, which is a misnomer; it is hard to find happiness in a drug-ridden neighborhood.

Pooh's wife showed up one day and was in the yard, screaming that it was wrong for him to be staying with me when she was his wife. She said that he could no longer visit with his baby until he came back to her. That was hard because he loved his son. So he went back to live with her but told me that he was living with his grandmother. I decided to get on with my life, but after about a week, he came back, saying that he missed me and the kids. I didn't take him back right away, but I finally gave in, and we moved to Alexander Court in Prichard.

This two-bedroom apartment was filled to the brim. By now, we had my sister's children as she was battling her drug addiction and HIV situation full-time. There were eight of us in the small space. God was always there for me when I had to deal with problems with my family. Some days, life was so difficult, but having Pooh's support was a blessing.

One day, we went to pick up his baby and go for a ride and were stopped by the police. Pooh had a warrant out for some back tickets, but he also had some weed in his pocket that I didn't know about. One of the cops said to let me go, but the other said, "No, let's check her out also." I also had a warrant for a back ticket as well.

Pooh begged them to let me go since we had his baby in the car and my children at home, but they wouldn't agree. I called my dad to help us out, and he said no, that he wouldn't help me sell drugs. I tried to convince him that it wasn't drugs on my part, but he wouldn't listen. They let Pooh sign for his own bond but wouldn't let me out because I didn't have enough money to pay for my cash bond.

I cried when he went out the door as he kept saying, "Baby, I will get out and come back to get you." He did. He went to my dad's house and convinced him to give us the rest of the money.

All of the time that we were together, his wife wouldn't consent to give him a divorce. Yes, I knew it was wrong for us to be together in the sight of God. We kept going to a lawyer, but nothing could be done, so we just stayed together for six years and went on with our lives.

We had lived on Pershing Drive in Prichard for about four years. A lot went on with my family during that time until I just wanted to give up on life. The depression got so bad that I wanted to kill myself. I went into the bathroom with a gun and pulled the handle back. Pooh came to the door and asked me what I was doing. Monica and I knew that God didn't want me to kill myself. That was the second time that I had attempted suicide. The first time, I took a lot of pills and blanked out, but when I woke up, I came back to myself.

he depression continued until July 13, 2003. I was alone in the house and went down on my knees and began to pray to God to help me. I was tired of living the life that I was living. I wanted better for me and my kids. All I remember is crying out to God and asking him to take over my life. I begged him to show me the way and kept repeating, "I need you, Lord, I need you."

When I looked up, the room was full of light. My body and everything felt different. My eyes were puffy, and tears were still running down my face, but I felt like a new person. Pooh asked me if I was okay because it looked like I had been crying. I told him that I was fine but that me and the Lord had a long time together. I asked him to look into the divorce again because I wanted to do what was right and in God's sight. But that never happened.

On July 21, 2003, around midnight, I had been in the bedroom, praying and reading the twenty-third Psalm. Every time that I got to "The Lord is my shepherd, I shall not want," I fell asleep. I did this about three times, and I walked through the house and checked on everyone when I thought that I smelled gas. I asked Pooh, and he said that he didn't smell anything, but I went into the kitchen, and the gas stove was turned on without the fire being lit. I asked Pooh if I could open a window to let the smell out, and he said no, it was too dangerous. I then asked him to put the youngest, baby doll, to bed because she was asleep in the living room in a chair by the front door. I heard him tell her to get up and go to bed, but she was too sleepy, so he took her to bed.

I then went back to reading the twenty-third Psalm again and fell asleep at least three times when I heard a loud noise that sounded like a gun had gone off. It wasn't unusual in this neighborhood to hear guns go off, so I tried to go back to sleep. But then I was startled and realized that that someone was shooting at our house. I got up and ran into the hall, and Sheetrock was falling, and the room was filled with smoke. All I remember was Pooh saying to get down, and all I can remember is trying to get to the kids and asking Pooh, "What have you done? What have you done to get someone this mad at you? Someone is trying to kill us!"

I kept hearing a still small voice saying over and over, "I got you, I got you." I could feel the bullets fly past me as I heard God's voice.

When the shooting stopped, and I was still standing, I could hear my grandmother's voice saying, "If you live for God, he will protect you."

The gunman had shot up my house with an AK-47 twenty-right times, and every wall, every bed had a hole in it. The only bullet that hit any of us was a small scrape on my son Terry's arm. The chair where my youngest had been sleeping had bullet holes through it. All I could do was say, "Thank you Lord" over and over. Hallelujah to God! I can't praise him enough. God's ministering angels put protection around each of us that night.

The police and detectives came, and one of them said, "I don't know who lives here, but if they don't know God, they need to get to know him because I have been in the field twenty years and have never seen anyone walk away alive like these people here."

I turned and looked at her and said, "I live here and know it was God who protected us."

We hugged and praised God together.

A neighbor finally told us that she saw the man shooting up our house that night, but she was afraid to report what she saw. She said that all she could think of was why someone would want to shoot up a house like that with people in it. The police didn't arrest anyone.

Of course, we had to move again. This time it was to Maysville. Pooh had moved back in with his mother until we could get married. We were determined to live for the Lord. Little did we know that we were moving right into the path of the gunman. On May 16, 2005, at about 8:00 a.m., the man shot and killed Pooh. Apparently, years before, the man had tried to rob Pooh, but Pooh shot him in self-defense and called the police. The man spent several years in jail, but when he got out, he was determined to get even. That was a sad day. All that I could think of was how someone could do that to another person. Pooh died at 8:35 a.m.

The neighbors reported that three cars pulled up, and after the first shot, one of went up to make sure Pooh was dead and shot him again.

The weekend before, Pooh was worried about getting my daughter, Terranika, to the prom on Friday night. He asked me to listen to a song called "I Tried" by the Geto Boys and "It's in My Heart to Serve the Lord" by Harvey Watkins. He had played hard with the kids all weekend, and before he left, he told me, "Baby, I am going to marry you to do right." The entire six years that we lived together, we kept saying that we would get married. But he was still legally married to his baby's mother.

The funeral was very difficult for me. When she showed up, I moved out of the way because that was the right thing to do. The newspaper read a devoted wife and then a devoted friend, Monica Lane. When my dad saw the paper, he called me and told me not to go to the funeral. I told him that in all respect that I had promised Michael J. Williams (Pooh) that I would always be there for him and I couldn't let him down now. My dad just didn't want me to be hurt any more than I was already.

The program for the funeral had her and her baby in the front and me and my children in the back. I certainly didn't like that because it looked like he was living a double life. We had been together for six years, but still, legally, she was his wife.

During this time, I was continuing to have some real problems with my oldest daughter. It wasn't anything that I wasn't used to, but it was very difficult living with her. She had a lying demon, and it was bad. I finally had to get the police involved, and her life was changed. Praise God for his intervention. I am glad that she made peace with Pooh before he got killed. I remember him telling her that he forgave her for what she had put us through and that he loved her.

It was hard living in that house after Pooh passed, so I moved back to Trinity Gardens across from my mom. That was a rude awakening when one of the saddest periods in my family would occur. My niece came to me about a problem that was going on in the family. She was living with my mom at the time. A pastor had told me that my sister's children needed me and that they already looked upon me as a mother figure. The preacher told me to let the Lord be the pilot in my life and me the copilot.

When my niece came to see me that day, I forgot all about that advice. When she asked me if she could come and live with me, I told her that she had her own room across the street and that my mom wouldn't let her live with me. She said again that Pooh had told her that we would take care of them, but I sent her back across the street.

Three days later, she was back again, asking for my help. I told her, "If I am going to help you, then you have to tell me what is going on."

She began to cry and said, "Auntie, don't make me go back. I am tired. That is my baby's daddy living with Grandmother."

Oh my God! It was like looking back into a mirror and seeing my self being molested at nine years of age, and no one was there to help. I was not going to let that happen to a family member again. I went to my mom and told her that she had twenty-four hours to give us the baby or I was calling the police.

The next day, I went to work and, at noon, called my niece and asked if she had gotten the baby, and she said no. I called the police and asked them to meet me at my mother's. They asked what the emergency was, someone was about to die. I told them just to meet me at her address.

About this time, my auntie called and asked what was going on and to stop causing trouble and leave my mom alone. I told her that there was a lot going on that she knew nothing about. I told her the curse of the sexual abuse in this family had to stop right now. First my sister, then me, and now my niece. My mom needed to tell the truth and admit to allowing this sin to happen. So now because of it, I would die trying to protect her.

I knew that I probably wouldn't have been able to keep the baby if I was in my niece's place, but she chose to keep him. When the police came, we were able to get the baby. I was so glad that God was able to keep me in my right mind, and my niece also. She is a strong black woman to be able to love that child, especially since he looked just like his father.

So now, my auntie and everyone else knew the truth of what was going on in my family for generations. All she could say was, "Lord have mercy."

I had an uncle who is passed now, but he wanted to kill the man for raping my niece. He would sit across the street and wait to see if the man was going to hurt us when he came in our yard. Life was difficult for quite a while.

My mom said that we had ruined her "happy home" and wouldn't talk to us for a long time. There wasn't anything ever happy about her home. The demon was playing all over it, and there was a lot of bad things going on. When you have a man looking at a child for sex, there is nothing good about that. I am so glad that God took over because I would have gone to jail for the rest of my life if I harmed that man the way that I wanted to.

t this time, I had been dating a guy named Chris Dozier. We had been dating a while, and he really pressured me to marry him, and I finally did. He was younger than me and quite handsome. It went well the first year and part of the second year. But then trouble started. He started playing around and messing with other women. So one day, he took me to work and had a wreck. We had to replace the car.

I had become friends with a lady from work who prefers to remain nameless in my story. She had told me months before that God had told her to adopt me as her goddaughter. She knew my sister, Della, and some of the background of our lives. She said that God wanted her to intervene in my life. At Christmas, she came into the hospital where I was working and gave me an envelope as a Christmas present.

She went back to her office, and I didn't open the envelope until I went to the restroom, and there was more than enough money for me and the kids to have a good Christmas. I could only praise Jesus, for he had blessed me again. God had sent me a new mama.

On the day that I decided that I had to buy a car, she called and asked how I was doing. I told her that I was at a car lot, trying to buy a car. She asked what car lot and insisted on coming out to help me. I tried to tell her that we would be okay, but she came anyway.

She picked out a car that was better than the one I had picked out, namely because it had a lot less miles on it. Then she cosigned for the loan. So I said that God had done it again.

When I got that car, all hell broke loose. Chris was mad because he didn't have a driver's license and couldn't get on the insurance, so he couldn't drive the car. He would slam the door so hard that I thought that the window would break, but thank God, it didn't. He was very jealous and never wanted me to talk to other men, yet he could talk to who he wanted to. He went to church with me three times the whole time we were together and to his grandmother's homecoming.

One day, he told me that this lady told him that he had fathered a little girl that was about seven or eight years old. I was shocked and said we had been together three years and asked where this child was. He wanted to bring her to spend the night with us, and I said no. After that, he said he needed time alone and moved in with his mother.

After about two weeks, he called me and said that he wanted us to talk about our marriage. He started telling me about how sorry he was about what he had done and wanted to move home. I was shocked when he told me that this lady was going to have a baby in three months and that it might be his. He said that if I didn't want him back, he would understand.

I had a whole three months to think about this and decide what to do. I let him come back and thought that things were going well until the baby was born. He came in and asked me if I wanted to go see the baby in the hospital. We got in his truck and went to Children's and Women's Hospital. The baby looked just like him. I walked out of the room, and a vision of the baby played in my head. He came after me and asked me why I left, and I said, "I wasn't there when you fathered this baby and I don't need to be here now."

I was mad all over again. As time passed, they would talk on the phone, and I knew that it wasn't just about the baby. She would call and ask for him to bring her something for the baby, but I knew that they were hooking up together again. We had to take a break from each other. He got a house with his brother.

One day, I went over to the house where he was staying because he said that he would help me move. He had already agreed that I would pick him up. I knocked on the door, and no one answered, even though I could hear movement inside. I went around to look in a window, but the window was too tall. I went back to knocking, and he came to the door, naked. I asked him why he was naked, and he said that was the way that he slept. I said, "You know that we are still married, and I know you." I tried to go in and see who he was with, but I couldn't get past him to see inside. He left with me and moved my things to the other house.

He came by several times in which he said that he only wanted to talk to me. One time, he tried to take my phone, and my daughter told him to leave or she would call the police. After about a month, we went on a date, and as we sat on the water, he said that he had been thinking about it and that he loved me and wanted to come back to me. He said that he didn't want to lose me.

I said, "It looks like that's what you want."

He said no and that he wanted to start over.

We decided to started over, and lo and behold, the next morning, not even a week later, he asked me to pay his cell phone bill. He had a meeting at work, and when he went into the meeting, I was preparing to pay his bill, and the phone rang. It was a lady asking to speak to Doziersack. I asked her to repeat what she said, and she asked me who I was. I told her that I was his wife, and she said her name was Brandy. I knew that she was the woman who had sent naked pictures to him last year, and he said that they were for his friend and her sister had sent them. He thought that I was some kind of fool to believe him.

She then said, "Oh, you're the wife. He told me that you would have to get a divorce before I could be with him. Oh, by the way, did he tell you that I am seven months pregnant and will be having his baby?"

I told her, "For once, what he told you will be true because you can have his ass." That was the second baby since we were married.

Never once did I ask God to get me out of the marriage because God wasn't the one who put me in it. So I kept the faith and got a divorce. I will never tell anyone that it was easy waiting on the process because it wasn't. I didn't have the money to pay for a divorce, but God made a way. I called my ex-mother-in-law, and she paid, even though she said that I shouldn't let those other women have him. I told her, "That is what he wants. He doesn't know how to be a husband, even though he told me multiple times that he didn't want a divorce."

When we went to the lawyer for the final papers, the lawyer asked who was going to pay the final bill. Chris said, "I am not paying because I don't want this divorce."

I said, "There is no final bill, it has been paid."

When we got outside, he said that he should slap me, and I said, "You didn't do that when we were married, and if you do, we will tear up downtown Mobile, baby. The least you can do is give me my name back. I deserve that, don't you think, Christopher?"

Life went on from there. I began to ask God not to let me hate Christopher or anyone. "I want to be able to love again, and right now, I need you, Lord, to be the head of my life."

After getting the divorce in 2011, God came into the scene again in 2012. At this time, my ex called me and said that they needed someone to clean the building that I used to help him clean. He had to go out of town for a while. The name of the company was Riteway Cleaning.

After I got married in 2008, I decided to go back to school to get my high school diploma. I took classes online. I had started back working at University Hospital in the kitchen again and started going to cosmetology school. I told the registrar that I had gotten my diploma online, and she said that she would check and for me to come back the next day. I did, and she said that everything was okay, and I went to school.

I did great. I had a 4.0 average. When I got close to the end of the program, I quit the hospital to be able to complete my hours by going to day and night classes.

About two weeks later, I got a call from the state board, and the lady said that I couldn't take the state board for cosmetology because I had gotten my diploma online. I got mad and asked her why they let me take and pay for all those classes. She began to tell me that I could take the GED or get proof that I had completed the tenth grade. I told her that with no disrespect, "But I just went through all this hard work for you to tell me this, really."

I cried out to the Lord for three days, "Oh, Lord, why is this happening to me right now?"

I went and talked to a lawyer, and she said that I had a case. I had to find work, so the lady that I had worked for Stanton Road Family Hair Care let me come and work for her in her shop. I thank God for her because she didn't have to do that. So I worked there for a while, then I moved my things and started working from home. I also cleaned the buildings and worked for Marshall Biscuit also.

After doing that for about two months, I told my third daughter, Terramisha, that I wasn't feeling well. She told me to go to the doctor, but I didn't want to go. The next day, I felt worse, and they took me to the doctor, and she sent me to the hospital. They did tests and told me everything was fine. But it wasn't. I couldn't go to work the next day. The pain in my stomach was so bad that I couldn't move. All I could do was pray to God and ask him what was wrong with me.

My kids called an ambulance, and I told them that I wasn't going. I went back to the doctor, and she sent me straight to the hospital again. She wanted me in the hospital because she didn't have the right equipment to test me properly.

It was my fortieth birthday, March 24, 2012. The kids brought me a cake, flowers, and balloons. I was smiling but was in a lot of pain. I asked the doctor not to give me anything for pain because I wanted to find out what was wrong with me. The meds weren't helping anyway. The pain got so much worse that I asked the Lord, "Take me, Lord. After the kids leave, take me home with you."

I knew that I had done everything that I could do, and the pain got worse every day. I kept hearing the Whitney Houston song "I Look to You." Every time that I would hear that song, I could hear God saying, "I got this." I kept praying that God had spared me from being raped at nine years of age, being shot at by an AK-47, and the many times that I could have been shot at the club, but I was going to die now because the doctors couldn't find anything wrong with me.

I started praying that when the doctors came in that Jesus would speak to them and lead them to the problem. I kept saying, "God, I look to you. Do it, Jesus, these are your hands. Find an answer."

The next time they came in, the main doctor examined me again and said, "I see the problem. We need to do surgery right away."

I remember saying, "Lord, thank you." If I could have gotten up, I would have hugged that doctor.

During the surgery, they gave me too much anesthesia. I could hear people talking and see them looking at me, but I couldn't respond. My family was hugging each other and crying. No one knew that I could see them but me and God. I started to pray for them, and I heard God say, "This is what you prayed for. See how it would be if you died."

I knew that God did not take me for a reason. I still had work to do on this earth. The next day, I came around, and one of the first people to see me was my ex, Chris. He said that someone told him that I was in the hospital, and he came to see if I was okay. I was still mad at him, but I asked God to heal me from all hurt. He helped me out of bed, and we walked and talked for about twenty minutes. I knew that I still loved this man but that I was not in love with him.

Something else that I remember from this time is while I was sick, my daughter had been cleaning the building that I was responsible for. The supervisor called and told me that I was fired from my job. She said that my daughter had been disrespectful to her, and they wanted the keys back from the building. I had a hard time believing that, but I had been very sick. The same daughter had been cleaning the building for me. The lady didn't know that she was talking to the person who had been doing the cleaning while I was ill.

After I went home from the hospital, I got a call from the manager of the company that I worked for. He said that he wanted to hear my side of the story. I told him that they thought that I was going to die, and the lady kept calling for the keys, and my daughter told her she didn't care and hung up on her. He told me that he was sorry that that had happened and that as soon as I was able that I would have my job back. God is good and will fight your battle every time. Just be still.

A few days after that, my angel called and told me that she had paid my car off. I tell you that I didn't know whether to cry, holler, or laugh. All I could do was say, "Thank you, Jesus!" God was working it all out on my sickbed. I know what God can and will do. He sent someone to bless me and my family. I could never repay God for what he does. I can only live right, obey his word, and be humble.

My brother told me about this guy that he worked with, and we share the same birthday, so I ended up going out with him. We were seeing each other for a while. Later in the year, I started praying and asking God if he was the right man for me. It turned out that he had gotten a woman pregnant, and she just seemed to pop up out of nowhere. I asked him if that was his baby that she was having, and he didn't answer me.

On New Year's Eve, I went to church, and after the service, I got a text from him, saying, "Happy New Year." On the way home, I saw his truck at the store on the corner and pulled up and could see the same woman in the truck. I pulled my car up so that he could see that I had seen him. I didn't say anything, but I did go around the block so that I could see them again. I called his phone, and he didn't answer.

The next day, he called me, and I didn't answer. He left a voice-mail and asked me to call him. He just wanted to know if I was all right.

I was hurt, and he knew it. I had a friend who had also seen them in the store together. I had to pray about this and have faith that I would get through this also. Like always, God doesn't make mistakes.

After that, my friend, Kissha, called when I was on the way to take one of my girls to college. She said that she knew this guy named Timothy who they called Tim, and she wanted me to meet him. He had asked for me to send a picture to her so that she could share it with him. He asked if he could call me, and I said yes. We went out on a date and talked for a while. We went out together for about two years. He seemed to be a nice guy. He treated me and my family nice.

Tim was with me when I got a call from the hospital. It was my sister, Della Mechelle. She had a seizure, and they left her in the house for three days before calling for help because she told them not to. He held me as I cried and told me that everything would be all right, but it wasn't. With him and my kids around me, I watched and prayed over her. Tim was right there with me. I was angry at myself and other people because I had tried to save her and couldn't.

We had this big sister and little sister thing, and I wasn't ready for her to die. I had prayed and prayed that the Lord would let her live. I knew that we all have to die someday, but I wasn't ready to let her go. We had only a little time to have fun. I asked God why so many things had to happen to me, and he said in his still small voice, "Why not you?"

I still was mad at God and asked for others to die in her place. But he had told me not to pray that selfish prayer anymore. I went into her room with a family friend, and when she left, I told Della that it was okay to rest in the Lord. "God and I have your kids. There is no need for anymore suffering and pain."

That was when I saw her arms and legs go up, and I knew that she was being freed from this land and into a better one. She was free at last. The next day, they took her off the ventilator, and she died on March 11, 2014. In my heart, I knew that she didn't have to battle her demons anymore. Her friend said that in the end that she refused to go to the hospital and refused for him to call anyone. She was ready to go.

I remember when Della had her fourth child, Lavarius (a.k.a. Lil' Man). The doctor told her that he had multiple problems and would never walk. He was also born with one kidney, and it wasn't working well. The doctors said his legs did not grow as they should. They had to break his little legs and put casts on them frequently. I had to help take him back and forth to Tulane hospital in New Orleans for treatment for about seven years. In between casts, he had to wear a brace. I kept him a lot during his early years due to Della's drug addiction and HIV status. At one point, he went to live with his mom for about six months, but when he got sick, she sent him back to me. Della's other children would come and go between me and their father or other family members. They certainly didn't have an easy life either.

After Della Mechelle died, Lil' Man was seventeen and was staying with me most of the time. For some reason, his dialysis treatments on Monday, Wednesday, and Friday were in Pensacola. I would take him back and forth, but it was difficult to get the money for the gas. But somehow, God always provided a way.

When he turned twenty-one, he was able to get a kidney transplant in Birmingham. We were praising God. Lil' Man has always been strong, even when he was small. After the transplant, something went wrong with the kidney. It was like a dream come true and a nightmare to follow. I took him to a hospital in Mobile, but no one would touch him. They said that he had to go back to UAB because that is who had done the surgery, and they were responsible for him. So they took him there, and he was in a very serious condition.

After we got there, no one was wanting to take the blame for what went wrong. I asked for the records and found out that the kidney they gave him had not been tested as it should have been before they gave it to him. So this was a big mess. Someone had dropped the ball big time.

Lil' Man had to go back on dialysis and wait for another kidney. In addition, he had to live with the infection that he got when he received the first kidney. He asked me, "Auntie, how can God bless you and then you be sicker than you were before you got the blessing?"

I told him, "Baby, just keep the faith, God makes no mistakes."

All his life, Lil' Man has fought for himself. We were told that he would never walk, but he can run faster than I can. I have seen it over and over. No one can tell me what God can't do. I have seen it over and over again. Thank you, Lord. Praises be to God.

I am a testimony to the fact that people can tell you anything when it comes to God and the Bible. The Bible says to study it yourself. Sometimes people say things to glorify themselves or simply to make money. I have been to many churches and listened to many sermons and testimonies. I take notes and go home and study them.

I have found that I need to depend on God and his Word instead of other people.

Relying on people, even ministers, can be dangerous; you never know their motives because Satan is a liar and deceiver and is willing to use anyone to spread evil. In the Bible, we learn about discernment and about false prophets. I have learned that my relationship to God is personal and to make that relationship grow. I have to read God's Word and pray daily. Turning my own way breaks that relationship, and sometimes, it is not easy to get back to where you should be.

I wake up every day, hoping to bless someone and live what I speak out of my mouth. If you are living your relationship to God, everyone will know it without you speaking a word. I thank God for what he is doing in my life. He isn't finished with me yet; my daily prayer is that someone can learn from my troubled life.

I remember having something called vertigo. At first, when I got dizzy at work, I thought it was my blood pressure, but it wasn't. When I would turn my head, the whole world would spin. I stayed home from work for three days, but I was still dizzy. I wouldn't wish this on anyone, but I learned later that most people get it from time to time.

One night, when I got out of the tub, I fell and hit my head. Blood was shooting everywhere. I called for my daughter and nephew, and they couldn't hear me. God finally gave me the strength to cry out louder, and my daughter heard me. She took me to the emergency room. While there, I kept my eyes closed so that the world would stay still. The cut was about two inches long, but from the amount of blood, you would have thought it was longer.

I was thinking about my life with God. My problems seem so big to me, but they are small to God. He can fix anything big or small. He will always be there for you. I am a testimony to the fact that he will be there for you if you serve him. All I can say is, "Thank you, God."

My entire life, I was told that I would never amount to anything other than a mother of a house full of kids. That hurts when it comes from someone you love. I started to live to prove her wrong. For a period of time, as a self-defense, I trained myself to not get close to anyone. And I did a great job of it. People would ask me why I was so mean. The only response that I had was, "Okay."

One of the men I dated said that I cut people off quick. After seeing them for a while, I would not respond to their calls. In my head, men were in the same category as my mother. They would only hurt you in the long run, so by avoiding people, I couldn't get hurt. I have learned that our heavenly Father God was an exception to this. I didn't have to prove anything to him. His love is complete.

The other exception was my children. I remember thinking that a mother's job is to protect her kids. I love them with all my heart and refuse to let them go through the neglect and abuse that I did. I always want them to know a mother's love. I know that sometimes I went too far in overprotecting them.

When Terranika was at Blount High School, twelve girls jumped her and beat her up. This was a continuation of fighting that had begun weeks earlier when they followed her home from school. It was like a nightmare when I got that call. Some of my children and friends had come to her defense. When they tried to send Nika and her cousin to the Youth Center, my husband at the time opened the door to the police car and told them to get out.

I was like an angry lion. I told them that I had been reporting the bullying they had been receiving for months and nothing had been done. The police told me that I was going to jail for interfering with the law. I told them they were defending themselves and if he wanted to arrest me, go ahead. I told them, "If you people had done something when I reported the problem, it would never had gotten this far. My child could have been killed by these bullies." They could see that I was very upset and realized that I was right.

I started to realize that they were grown when they started telling me to go and live my life. They all know the type of childhood that I had and know that it is time that I did something for myself.

I never had a loving birth mother, but I have had a few loving mothers anyway. My stepmother, Annie King, treats me and my kids as if we were her own. She has told me many times how much she loves me. I have another mother figure, Mrs. Annie Watkins, who loves me completely. I have another mother who doesn't want to be named but has loved me completely. I love her as I would a birth mother. I had prayed for a mother my entire life, and God had given me several. You don't have to be related by blood to have or give a mother's love; it can be people God puts in your life.

Thank you, God, for all you do for me and my kids. According to the Bible, we originally come from dirt. I know that good things come from dirt because look at me. I am a pearl now that God created from dirt placed in an unreal environment.

A pearl is a hard mass produced in the shell of a mollusk after having a piece of dirt inserted into it. Pearls come in many colors, but white, black, green and pink are the most common colors. Unlike gems, which are usually formed in the earth itself, pearls are formed from a living creature. So that is what God has done in my life. I am a brown pearl created from a dark heart and messed up person.

I looked up *dirt,* and it is defined as a collection of smashed rocks, clay, silt, sand, and plants. That dirt is different every few ways depending on the composition of which it is made up of. Sometimes we look at dirt as dark and ugly. Other times, it is beautiful, bringing new life to plants. Some of my life is like a pile of dirt. When I look back over my life, I see that I am like that dirt. With God's love, prayer, and service to him, I have grown just like a flower. God is my foundation and has given me the water, sunshine, and fertilizer to let me bloom. Just like a flower, it takes time for a change in our lives. Our lives are not like a microwave. We have to be slowly baked, mixed, and heated to reach our best. But unlike plants and baked goods, we have to be willing to accept God's blessings.

God is so good. Every time we fall, he is there to pick us up and replant us in his love. He tells us to keep on pushing upward toward him.

This is a true story of a life, a traumatic story of neglect, abuse, betrayal, murder, and survival. God has transformed my life. The reason that I have written it is so that people can see that God can make a pearl out of dirt if you follow him. Psalm 23 is the scripture that has led me through the valley of death and let me lie down in the green pastures. Praise be to God.

ABOUT THE AUTHOR

Monica La-sha Lane was born on March 24, 1972, in Mobile, Alabama, to Eddie Mae Lane and Judge King Jr. Monica has five kids, and she also helped raise her sister's kids. Monica has five grandkids and one on the way. Monica loves her family and would do all she can to make sure they're okay.

She enjoys looking at the water and she loves the outdoors. Monica loves God most of all. Monica went back to school in 2009 and received her high school diploma, and one year after, she went to cosmetology school and got her diploma. She loves helping people and doing hair.

Monica has worked as a CNA/Caregiver in the past, and she worked at three different hospital. She also worked at a plant, packing bread, and as a machine operator for about fourteen years. She always says her true calling is doing hair, making people look nice and feel good about themselves.

Monica now works at Allied Universal Security, and she is still serving people. Monica also has a personal hair salon in loving memory of her sister, Della M. Lane, who passed on March 11, 2014. Monica always keeps her faith in God, no matter what she is going through. She loves Psalm 23. Her favor quote: *God is love.*